Under His Wings

Tempest

Discovering God's Presence in the Midst of Storms

(A Study of Psalm 55)

Written by Martha Streufert Jander
Edited by Laine Rosin

Concordia Publishing House

Editorial assistant: Laura Christian

Copyright © 1999 by Concordia Publishing House
3558 South Jefferson Avenue, St. Louis, MO 63118-3968
Manufactured in the United States of America

Contents

Session 1   5

    David Faces Tempest and Storm

Session 2   12

    Storms for the Woman at the Well

Session 3   19

    Martha's Storms

Session 4   26

    God's Presence in the Midst of Storms

David Faces Tempest and Storm

Where Are We Going?

We will identify and discover causes of storms in our life; look at the storm David was facing and see what he did about it; use Psalm 55 and related texts to call on God in the midst of storms, knowing that He hears and answers.

Ready, Set, Go

Begin with prayer. Turn yourself over to God. Ask for the power of His Holy Spirit to lead you through the study so that you can "weather the storms in your life" and know that God is there with you in the midst of them.

Spend a few minutes on **"Where Am I Now?"** Picture the storms in your life at the present time. Get into **"The Search,"** writing your thoughts in the spaces provided. As you study the psalm, find God's presence in the midst of your own storms. He is there to calm and bless.

Take time to **"Respond,"** seeking God in the midst of the tempests you face, using the psalm to realize His gift of peace in His presence. Then place yourself into God's strong arms in prayer.

Before the next session, do the **"Do,"** recording your thoughts and experiences in the journal page following this session, filling in the prayer page (or using it as a way to pray each day).

Where Am I Now?

Discuss the worst weather storm you ever experienced. Then respond:

How strong are the storms of life you face today?
- Not—the sun is shining brightly
- A gentle shower
- A steady downpour
- A dense fog
- A thunderstorm with dark clouds and lightning flashes
- An icy blizzard with slippery slopes
- A hurricane or tornado with damaging winds

The Search

The Storms of Betrayal

1. David wrote Psalm 55 at the time Absalom was leading a rebellion against him. Having his own son take up arms against him broke a torrent of feelings in David (Psalm 63), but on top of that was the wrenching discovery of a close friend's betrayal. Ahithophel had been David's advisor and counselor (2 Samuel 16:23). Read about his betrayal in 2 Samuel 15:10–12 and 30–37. Briefly describe David's situation.

Fleeing from Tempest and Storm

2. Read all of Psalm 55. Then look more closely at verses 1–5. How does David describe the storms in his life?

3. What happens to a relationship when trust is betrayed? Have you ever been betrayed or disappointed by a friend, relative, coworker? What was your reaction? How did you deal with your feelings? What word pic-

tures can you use to describe what you were going through?

4a. Read verses 6–8. What did David long for? Could he outrun the storms?

4b. To keep Jerusalem from having a bloodbath and the people there from suffering, David chose to flee into the wilderness, perhaps not running away from trouble as much as running toward God's refuge. What is your reaction when storms of life overwhelm you? Why can't we outrun those storms? What happens when we try?

God's Refuge

5. David wanted refuge, and he also wanted Ahithophel's advice to come to nothing. Read verses 9–11. In these verses David calls down God's wrath on his enemies, especially on his betrayer. David wanted evil destroyed and God's plan for the kingdom of Israel and the kingdom of God to succeed. 2 Samuel 5:1–4 tells us that God had chosen David to be king over Israel, and in 1 Kings 1:28–31 and 3:7 we find that Solomon was to be his successor. Absalom was not only defying his father, the king, but also God's plan for the kingdom of Israel. What is God's plan for your life? What evil sometimes gets in the way of God's fulfilling His plan for you and for His kingdom through you?

6a. In verse 19 of the psalm, David indicates that evil people do not change. They thwart God's plans and plot the overthrow of God's people. David wanted the speech and advice of his enemies confused so that their plans—against God's anointed—would come to naught. Read verses 16–23. What did David know about God? Why could David so confidently put his trust in God?

6b. What do you know about God? Why can you confidently put your trust in Him?

7. When your sin overwhelms you, when you are thrown into disorder with your tasks, or when you feel overcome by an enemy or crushed by the wickedness of others, you too can pray that evil will be destroyed and that God's plan for you and for His kingdom will succeed. You can confess your sins, knowing that Jesus paid the cost on the cross. You can pray for God's Spirit to convict others of their sin and turn them to His saving grace. How else can you pray for yourself? for your enemies?

Respond

God responded to David's needs. He brought Ahithophel's plan to ruin (2 Samuel 15:31–37; 17:1–5, 14) and when Ahithophel saw Absalom's defeat, he went home and hanged himself (2 Samuel 17:23). This is not how we want our enemies' lives to end, but we do want evil to come to an end. Be certain that it is God who will bring it to an end—that is not our job. God sent Jesus to defeat evil and rob it of its fatal power, which He did on the cross. And while the storm clouds of evil may break over our heads, we can pray, "When my heart is overwhelmed; Lead me to the rock that is higher than I" (Psalm 61:2 NKJV). And we can know that God, the rock of our salvation, is with us and will save us.

Once again read Psalm 55:15–23. Then pair up with a partner and read verse 22 to one another, ending with a paraphrase of the last part of verse 23: "And as for you, [person's name], you can trust in God."

Pray together, expressing concerns brought out in the study, encouraging each other to pray. Ask for God's assurance of His presence, His peace, His forgiveness. Then praise Him for His faithfulness, mercy, and love.

Do

This week be aware of times when the storms of life gather over your head. Record these times in the journal page that follows. Ask the Lord to show you the cause of the storms and, if they are caused by sin, to forgive you or forgive others through you. Ask God for the assurance of His peace and presence during these times, knowing that He is faithful to His promises, that He does not forsake us or leave us to struggle on our own.

Additional Bible readings for this week: Genesis 28:10–22; Isaiah 43; and Matthew 8:23–27. Copy and attach to a mirror or other place you see daily the words of Deuteronomy 31:6.

Use the prayer starters each day as you come to the Lord in your quiet time, either writing in your own endings to the sentences or leaving them blank to be used in a new way each day.

For next week, read in John 4:3–43 about the woman at the well and the burden she carried. Read through and think about Session 2, filling in any responses as you like.

Journal Page

_____

_____

_____

_____

_____

_____

_____

_____

_____

_____

_____

_____

_____

_____

_____

_____

_____

_____

_____

_____

_____

_____

_____

_____

_____

_____

_____

O Lord, You are so _____

_____

_____

_____

and I am so _____

_____

_____

_____

Please forgive me for _____

_____

_____

_____

_____

Help me _____

_____

_____

_____

_____

Please bless and take care of _____

_____

_____

_____

_____

Thanks, Lord, for _____

_____

_____

_____

_____

Storms for the Woman at the Well

Where Are We Going?

We will look at how sin causes storms in our life; at the storm the woman at the well was facing and see what Jesus did about it; and reflect on Psalm 55 to see how God removes the storms of sin with His saving grace.

Ready, Set, Go

Begin with prayer. Invite the Holy Spirit to open your mind and heart to His teachings and comfort as you learn from God's Word. Ask Him to help you see that God is bigger than your biggest storms and that His weakness is stronger than your might.

Take a few minutes to answer **"Where Am I Now?"** As you do **"The Search,"** discuss and write your responses in the spaces provided. As you study, discover God's forgiving love and the results of His mercy.

Wind up your study with **"Respond,"** knowing God blesses those who gather in His name. Then pray together, seeking His refuge from your storms and opening your hearts to His healing love.

During the next week, do the "**Do**," recording your thoughts and experiences in the journal page following this session, filling in the prayer page (or using it as a way to pray each day).

Where Am I Now?

Think back to a time in your "middle" childhood (ages 8 to 12). If you feel comfortable doing so, discuss with a small group the biggest storm you faced at that time.

The Search
Jesus and the Woman at the Well

Jesus walked through Samaria. This was unusual because no Jew deliberately chose that road from Judea to Galilee, going instead the "long way around," traveling across the Jordan and up the east side. But Jesus had a mission. "He *needed* to go through Samaria" (John 4:4 NKJV, emphasis added). This need included a woman. Read about her in John 4:6–26.

1a. Why did this woman come to the well in the middle of the day rather than in the cool of the evening when she would have had other women for companionship? What storms was this woman facing? Do you suppose she ever thought, "Oh, that I had the wings of a dove! I would fly away and be at rest" (Psalm 55:6)?

1b. What storms are you facing that might cause you to say, "Oh, that I had the wings of a dove! I would fly away and be at rest" (Psalm 55:6)? Answer in this space or in the quietness of your heart.

2a. What did Jesus know about the woman? What did He want her to know about Him in the midst of her storm? about God? How did Jesus show that He loved this woman and that He cared about her daily life and her spiritual life?

2b. Why has God chosen you? What does He know about you? How has He shown His love for you and that He cares about your daily life and your spiritual life?

The Storms of Sin

3. Sin separates us from God and, as in the case of the woman in John 4, from other people as well. When has sin separated someone you know from God's love and from yours? When has sin separated you from God or from others?

4. Sin and its consequences can leave us in a vacuum—both spiritually and socially. We may avoid others and tell ourselves they are snubbing us. We may ignore God's Word, thinking it will only condemn us. We may avoid worship and the Lord's Supper, believing we are unworthy. What have been your reactions to sin in your own life? (Answer this, if you prefer, in the quietness of your own heart.)

5a. In verse 10, Jesus says, "If you knew the gift of God and who it is that asks you for a drink ..." God's gift is no less than His grace to us shown in Christ Jesus, a gift paid for by Jesus' suffering and death on the cross, a gift God gives freely. The woman at the well expected no love or care from her neighbors, much less from a stranger. Jesus knew all about her (vv. 17–18). Witness her astonishment (v. 19). Yet, Jesus offered her the quenching love of God's forgiveness, "a spring of water welling up to eternal life" (v. 14). Why do you suppose she was so eager (at first) to have the "living water" Jesus offered (v. 15)? What do you think the real living water meant to the woman? Read John 4:28–29. What was the woman's reaction to Jesus' gift?

5b. Jesus knows all about us too. Nothing is hidden from Him. And Jesus offers that same redeeming fountain to us. He offers it in His Word, in the bread and wine of His Holy Supper. Through His death on the cross He gives us eternal life, abundant life. Through His gift we are made alive in Him, made clean in His blood—from the inside out. All our sin and guilt are washed away. What does this gift mean to you? What is your response to it?

6a. Read Psalm 55:16–18, then John 4:39–42. How had the woman's situation changed? How had her neighbors changed? What made the difference?

6b. When and how has God Himself been a refuge in the storms of your life? How has God changed your situations through His forgiving love? How has He changed you?

Respond

The woman was so excited about her new relationship with God that she just had to tell someone—and she tells the very neighbors who, for all we know, had snubbed her with veiled looks or pointing fingers. Many of them came to believe in Jesus too, not just on her testimony, but because they heard and saw for themselves that this was the Christ, "the Savior of the world." What a sound of song and praise must have arisen from the little Samaritan village of Sychar when Jesus left them with the spring of living water.

Together, sing a song of praise or pair up and choose from among these Bible selections to read to one another: Psalm 65; Psalm 66; or Isaiah 12, substituting your partner's name when suitable.

Pray as a large group, praising God for His love and His spring of water, welling up to eternal life. Encourage one another to come before God's throne of mercy, speak to Him as His own children, and bring to Him concerns mentioned in today's study.

Do

During this next week, use your journal page to record times that you are stormed by sin—your own or of others. Reread the story of the woman at the well. Then go to God in prayer, knowing that He hears and answers for the sake of His Son, Jesus, who took all your sins to the cross and rose victorious over sin, death, and the devil.

Additional Bible readings include Psalm 130; John 8:2–20; and Romans 8. Copy the words of 1 John 3:20 and place it on your mirror or other place where you will see it often.

Use the prayer starters each day as you come to the Lord. Fill in the blanks with various endings, or leave them empty to use the starters fresh each day.

For next week, read Luke 10:38–42 to review the story of Martha and the burden she carried. Read through and think about Session 3, filling in any responses as you like.

Journal Page

O Lord, You are so _____

_____

_____

_____

and I am so _____

_____

_____

_____

Please forgive me for _____

_____

_____

_____

Help me _____

_____

_____

_____

Please bless and take care of _____

_____

_____

_____

Thanks, Lord, for _____

_____

_____

_____

Session 3

Martha's Storms

Where Are We Going?

We will study the storm in Martha's life and how Jesus showed it for what it really was; then look to see how Jesus brings us relief from the storms in our lives with His presence and the power of His Word.

Ready, Set, Go

Begin with prayer. Praise God for bringing you together with others to study His Word. Ask for the power and wisdom that only the Holy Spirit can give as He opens your heart to understanding and joy.

Take time to do the "**Where Am I Now?**" and encourage one another to discuss and share. Then get into "**The Search**," exploring the message of God's Word for you and discovering how He waits to fill you with His love and joy as He relieves the storms of your own making from your life.

Spend a few minutes on "**Respond**," envisioning what God wants for you and praying together in the strong name of Jesus.

Before the next session, do the "**Do**," recording your thoughts and experiences in the journal page following this session, filling in the prayer page (or using it as a way to pray each day).

Where Am I Now?

Describe a time in your teen years when your parents, teachers, or other adults expected certain things from you. Tell what these expectations were and if and how they caused storms in your life. Looking back as an adult, would you consider these reasonable or unreasonable expectations?

The Search

The Visit

Martha, Mary, and their brother Lazarus lived in the little village of Bethany, an easy walk of about two miles from the city of Jerusalem. From all indications, Martha was the elder daughter, in charge of the household and the servants and, as we see in the text, wanting charge of her siblings. Martha's home seemed to be a favorite stopping place for Jesus—a quiet place where He could go with His disciples to get a good meal and have good conversation with the sisters and brother.

1a. On this visit, Martha took on the responsibility of the kitchen. She most likely figured that Jesus and His friends had been walking and working and now needed food. And so she began preparing a meal. Read Luke 10:38–42. What are some things Martha might have done before she spoke to Jesus to let Mary know that she needed help? How might she have shown her displeasure over her sister's choice? How does Martha indicate by what she says that she might have even been upset with Jesus?

1b. Describe what you feel or do when you see people not carrying their fair share of the work. How do you sometimes respond when no one notices how much work you are doing? What are your feelings at these times?

2a. Look carefully at the first few words of verse 40. How was Martha reacting to the preparations *she had chosen to do?* What were Martha's expectations of herself when Jesus and His entourage appeared? of Mary? of Jesus? What words from Psalm 55 might Martha have used to express her feelings?

2b. When you are "distracted by all the preparations," what expectations do you have of yourself? of others? How do you perceive others' expectations of you? Are they actual or only what you think others expect?

3. It might be easy to side with Martha when we know how much work it is to prepare a meal, even with all our conveniences, and knowing she faced unexpected company of perhaps 13 hungry men. Shouldn't Mary have been helping? Shouldn't Jesus have told Mary, "Your sister needs you. Run along and help. We can talk later"? What is your reaction to Jesus' scolding Martha?

Now read carefully Jesus' words to Martha in verse 41: "you are *worried and upset* about many things" (emphasis added). Jesus was not putting Martha down for wanting to prepare and serve a meal. He certainly was not chastising her for the work she was doing. Rather, He was telling her, "Martha, put first things first. When you choose to hear My Word, then you can go about your work with a singing heart. God's love revealed to you in My Word will remove any storm that you yourself have caused. Then your work will not be a yoke around your neck but a service of joy."

Martha's storm was not one of sin, though it led to sin. (Which sin?) It was not even a storm of service or one that anyone had required or asked of her. It was instead one she had caused herself, in a sense showing others around her, "See how busy I am serving Jesus. Look at all I am doing for Him." But Jesus asked of her only one thing, that she should choose, like Mary, to sit and listen to Him, to bask in the warmth of His love and drink of His living water.

The Burden Lifted

4. Write an ending to Martha's story. Imagine what she did after Jesus spoke to her. Make it an ending that shows how Jesus changed Martha's heart and gave her a willing spirit to listen to His Word. (Read Martha's confession of faith in John 11:24.)

5. Read David's words in Psalm 55:22. How can sitting at Jesus' feet give us refuge from the storms of life and make the storms we sometimes cause ourselves to melt like mist in the morning sun? Why is putting aside a time each day to delve into God's Word vital to your spiritual welfare? What can Jesus do for you as you daily steep yourself in His Word? as you weekly worship Him in church? as you often partake of the Lord's Supper?

Respond

In Matthew 11:28–30, Jesus says, "Come to Me, all you who are weary and burdened, and I will give you rest. Take My yoke upon you and learn from Me, for I am gentle and humble in heart, and you will find rest for your souls. For My yoke is easy and My burden is light." Give Jesus the things that cause storms in your life— your expectations of yourself and of others; the petty grievances you have against a spouse, a child, a friend, a coworker; the little things that annoy and confuse and confound you. Jesus does not want you whirled away by these things any more than He wants you to be knocked down by the storms sin causes, storms He removed by His death on the cross. He can and will be your refuge in *every* storm. He is faithful. He loves you.

Today in small groups of three or four, pray for the person on your right, asking God to reveal His refuge for that person in the storms she is facing (it isn't necessary to name them specifically). If you feel comfortable doing so, lay a gentle hand of blessing on the head or arm of that person as you pray. Then together, bring to God any other concerns that have been expressed during this time.

Do

During this next week, record on the journal page times that you are buffeted by the storms of guilt, stress, and heaviness of heart and also of times you cause the storms. Then give them to God in prayer, knowing He is our refuge in all storms and that He sent Jesus to remove the effects of the storms of sin when He went to the cross. Now in joy we are able to serve Him and others.

Bible readings this week: Exodus 3:1–10; Psalm 55; Isaiah 55; and Hebrews 12:1–2. Copy the words of Matthew 11:28–30 on a piece of paper and attach it where you will see it often.

Use the prayer starters each day as you come to the Lord in the midst of your storms, either writing in endings to each one or using them fresh each day.

Read through Session 4 for next week, filling out any answers as you wish.

Journal Page

_____
_____
_____
_____
_____
_____
_____
_____
_____
_____
_____
_____
_____
_____
_____
_____
_____
_____
_____
_____
_____
_____
_____
_____
_____
_____

O Lord, You are so _____

_____

_____

and I am so _____ :

_____

_____

Please forgive me for _____ :

_____

_____

Help me _____

_____

_____

_____

Please bless and take care of _____

_____

_____

_____

Thanks, Lord, for _____

_____

_____

_____

_____

Session 4

God's Refuge; God's Victory

Where Are We Going?

We will take a deeper look today at Psalm 46 to discover the quietness of God; to find out how we can be still and know that God is God; to exalt God as our strength and fortress.

Ready, Set, Go

Begin with prayer. Ask God to come to you in the quietness of your study, to open His Word to you through His Spirit so that you might know that He is God.

Spend a few minutes on **"Where Am I Now?"** Think about the quiet times of your day. Get into **"The Search."** Dig into the Word, ready to have God reveal His strength and power in it for you.

Take time to **"Respond,"** concentrating on God and who He is. Then pray together, lifting your hearts and voices to the Lord.

Before the next session, do the **"Do,"** recording your thoughts and experiences in the journal page following this session, filling in the prayer page (or using it as a way to pray each day).

Where Am I Now?

Describe the quietest part of your day. On a scale of 1 to 10, with 1 being the quietest and 10 the loudest, mark on the chart where your mornings are (A.M.); your afternoons (P.M.); your evenings (E); and your nights (N). Spend a few minutes discussing why you placed your marks as you did.

1	2	3	4	5	6	7	8	9	10

The Search
A Teaching Psalm

1a. Psalm 55 is called a *maskil*, meaning a teaching psalm, one that instructs. Looking back over the past three sessions, what did the people studied (David, the woman at the well, Martha) discover about themselves as they were beset by storms? What did they learn about God as they confronted Him—or as He confronted them? about God's redeeming work in Jesus? Check your notes or the Bible references from those sessions.

1b. Read the psalm aloud meditatively. As you do so, jot down things that (1) God may be teaching you about yourself; (2) God may be teaching you about Himself; (3) God may be teaching you about His redemptive work through the promised Savior.

2a. Now look closely at verses 1–3. What is the first thing David asked God? What does this show about David? about his relationship with God? about his prayer life? How did the woman at the well and Martha begin to see that Jesus was their refuge in times of storm?

2b. Where can you too go when the storms of life come upon you? Why can you trust that God will be with you, that He will hear and answer your cry?

3a. Quietly read verses 4–8 to yourself. Then briefly reflect how David, the woman at the well, and Martha all had cause or thought they had cause to want to "fly away and be at rest." How would you describe your longing for peace in the midst of storms? What did God reveal about Himself to each of them?

3b. Storms threaten our safety and security. They would "blow us away." Storms threaten our security with God and would blow us out of the safe haven of His arms. What have you learned about the storms in your life? How has God shown Himself to you in recent storms?

4a. Look again at verses 9–15. Recall David's situation and the evil that surrounded him. What evil were the woman at the well and Martha facing?

4b. What evil do you encounter today? What evil threatens God's church on earth? How can you pray? What can you pray God to do in the midst of evil? to do about the evil?

5a. Reread verses 16–19a. What do these verses teach you about God? about yourself?

5b. Jesus fought our biggest battle—the war waged against the devil, the world, and our own sinful flesh—when He suffered on the cross for our sins. He died victorious, for God had demanded a blood sacrifice for our redemption, and that is the price Jesus paid. But Jesus also rose victorious, showing death and the devil once and for all that they had no power over Him—and over those for whom He had gone to the cross. Since Jesus defeated death and the devil, know for a certainty that He will also join in your battles against them. You are God's child, and He does not want to see you beaten down and destroyed. The words of verse 16 are written in the present tense. God's saving is an ongoing, ever-present occurrence. What are some things from which God has saved you in the past? From what is He working to save you now?

6. Read verses 19b–21. Is evil always readily seen as evil? How can evil disguise itself?

Through His Word, God helps us to be aware of evil and its true intent. He gives us the wisdom to see evil for what it is, and He assures us of His own power over and defeat of evil.

7. Read again verses 22–23. Underline verse 22. You are righteous before God because of Jesus Christ. He has given you His righteousness by Jesus' death and resurrection, and in this verse He promises that He will not let you fall. He is your strength, your refuge in the midst of storms. Why is this important for you to know?

Respond

Verse 6 of the psalm says, "Oh, that I had the wings of a dove! I would fly away and be at rest." But in Isaiah 40:31, God tells us, "Those who hope in the LORD will renew their strength. They will soar on wings like eagles; they will run and not grow weary, they will walk and not be faint." God gives us the wings of an eagle. He gives us His strength by the power of His Spirit to face into the storm or to soar above and beyond the storms of life to His safe and secure haven.

Write a prayer, poem, or just a few words that reflect how God has worked in your faith and life in the past few weeks to help you grow and mature in your understanding and awareness of God's presence in the midst of your storms.

Pray together as a group, encouraging one another as you bring your concerns to God's throne of grace, confident that you can trust in Him.

Do

Continue to express your thoughts and reflections in the journal page. Earnestly seek God's help in the midst of storms and record His response to you.

For further reading this week, look at Psalm 21; Isaiah 40; and John 14. Copy the words of John 14:14 on a piece of paper and attach it to a mirror or other place you see often.

Discover God's abiding love for you as you use the prayer starters to record your own prayers or to pray each day.

Journal Page

O Lord, You are so _____

_____

_____

_____

and I am so _____

_____

_____

_____

Please forgive me for _____

_____

_____

_____

_____

Help me _____

_____

_____

_____

_____

Please bless and take care of _____

_____

_____

_____

_____

Thanks, Lord, for _____

_____

_____

_____

_____

O Lord, You are so

and I am so

Please forgive me for

Help me

Please bless and take care of

Thanks, Lord, for

Under His Wings

Refuge

Becoming Aware of God in All Phases of Our Lives

(A Study of Psalm 46)

Written by Martha Streufert Jander
Edited by Laine Rosin

CPH®
Concordia Publishing House

Editorial assistant: Laura Christian

Contents

Session 1   5
> God's Victories for His People

Session 2   12
> Anna's Refuge

Session 3   19
> Martha's Refuge

Session 4   26
> God's Refuge; God's Victory

God's Victories for His People

Where Are We Going?

We will look at God's victories for His servant
Jehoshaphat and see how this king was aware of God's
presence in the midst of attack, and how God works in
our lives so we become more aware of His presence.

Ready, Set, Go

Begin with prayer. Ask for God's Spirit to bless your
study of His Word and to open your eyes to the victories He has brought to your life.

Spend a few minutes on **"Where Am I Now?"** Think
about the victories God gives in your life. Get into **"The
Search,"** writing your thoughts in the spaces provided.
As you study the psalm, concentrate on seeing God
active in your own life.

Take time to **"Respond,"** praising God for being
your refuge and strength. Then place yourself into God's
strong arms in prayer.

Before the next session, do the **"Do,"** recording your
thoughts and experiences in the journal page following
this session, filling in the prayer page (or using it as a
way to pray each day).

Where Am I Now?

Where do you see God's victories in your life?

____ Relationships	____ Self-control
____ Bible study and prayer	____ Patience
____ Faithful worship	____ Not holding grudges
____ Forgiving others	____ Selflessness
____ Overcoming pride	____ Other: _____

The Search
God's Victory for Jehoshaphat

While many psalms record authors and respond to specific situations, others seem to have been written for general use for different events. Psalm 46 is one of those psalms. However, for the purpose of this study we will look at the psalm in regard to the victory of God through His servant Jehoshaphat.

Jehoshaphat was a king of Judah who "did what was right in the eyes of the LORD" (1 Kings 22:43). Not only was Jehoshaphat aware of God's presence in his life, but during his reign, the Levites "taught throughout Judah, taking with them the Book of the Law of the LORD; they went around to all the towns of Judah and taught the people" (2 Chronicles 17:9). Indeed, "The fear of the LORD fell on all the kingdoms of the lands surrounding Judah, so that they did not make war with Jehoshaphat" (17:10).

1a. But 2 Chronicles 20 records an unexpected cloud on Jehoshaphat's peaceful horizon. Read verses 1–2 to see what happened to disturb the calm. Then read verses 3–13 to see the king's immediate response to the trouble. What surprises you about these verses? How does Jehoshaphat acknowledge God? How does this text show his utter trust and reliance on the Lord?

1b. What is your first reaction to trouble that disturbs your peace? How would your family or friends describe how you face crises? What victories do you need in your life?

2a. List the things Jehoshaphat reminded God about in these verses. Why do you suppose he did that?

2b. List things that God has done for you (see "Where Am I Now?"). Be specific in your answers. What can result when you remember these things?

3a. Jehoshaphat says in the last part of verse 12, "We do not know what to do, but our eyes are upon You." After reminding the Lord of things that He had done for His people, the king admits his inadequacy—and the inadequacy of the people—in facing this "vast army." Name other times in biblical history where God's people were totally inadequate to overcome the challenges or fears that faced them and how God responded to their need.

3b. When have you felt yourself to be totally inadequate in situations where there seemed to be no way out? What was your reaction? How did God respond to your need?

The Victory Is the Lord's

4a. Read 2 Chronicles 20:14–19 to see what the Lord's answer to Jehoshaphat was. Then read verses 20–30 to find out how God carried out His plan. What a battle plan! What a victory! Why do you think God chose this way in which to defeat the enemy? What did God ask Jehoshaphat and the people to do?

4b. What do you suppose happened to the relationship between God and His people as a result of this victory?

5. Finish this sentence, then tell what can happen to your relationship with God as a result of His help: "If God gave that kind of victory to Jehoshaphat and the people of Judah, here is what God can do for me ..." (See your answer to question 1b.)

The Lord Almighty Is with Us

6a. Now read Psalm 46. This is a psalm that Jehoshaphat and the people of Judah could very easily have prayed as they marched from Jerusalem and as they returned. What verses especially reveal that? How did God show to His people that He should be "exalted among the nations ... in the earth"?

6b. How does God show His people today that He is "exalted among the nations ... in the earth"?

6c. In what ways has God revealed Himself to you, that He is with you, that He is your refuge?

Respond

God gave victory to Jehoshaphat and His people in a unique way. God's greatest rescue for us comes through His Son, Jesus, who on the cross won the victory over sin and Satan. With the banner of Christ raised high, we can march through life, winning victories through His power and in His name. Choose a verse from Psalm 46 and tell what it can mean for you in your life this week. Read the entire psalm in unison, sharing Bibles that have the same version if necessary.

Then pray together, lifting up your needs and concerns to the Lord, giving Him praise for the victories that are already yours through the power of His Spirit.

Do

This week ask the Lord to open your eyes to let you see the victories that He accomplishes for you and through you. Record these in your journal and praise God for being your refuge and strength. When you seem to fall into "the heart of the sea" and there is roaring and foaming and quaking all about you, be assured that the God of Jacob is with you, that He is your refuge, that He gives victories to you for the sake of Jesus.

Additional Bible readings for this week: Psalm 118; Isaiah 42:1–9; and 1 John 5:1–5. Copy and attach to a mirror or other place you see daily the words of a verse of Psalm 46 that reminds you of God's victories in your life.

Use the prayer starters each day as you come to the Lord in your quiet time, either writing in your own endings to the sentences or leaving them blank to be used in a new way each day.

For next week, read about Anna in Luke 2:36–38. Read through and think about Session 2, filling in any responses as you like.

Journal Page

O Lord, You are so _____

_____

_____

_____

and I am so _____

_____

_____

_____

Please forgive me for _____

_____

_____

_____

_____

Help me _____

_____

_____

_____

v _____

Please bless and take care of _____

_____

_____

_____

_____

Thanks, Lord, for _____

_____

_____

_____

_____

Session 2

Anna's Refuge

Where Are We Going?

We will look at Anna, who spoke to Mary and Joseph about the Child Jesus. She was confident in God's love for her and in His promise of salvation. We will grow in an awareness of God's presence in our lives as our refuge at all times and in all situations.

Ready, Set, Go

Begin with prayer. Ask the Lord to bless your study of His Word as He makes you aware of His presence in your life.

Spend a few minutes on "**Where Am I Now?**" and describe a safe fortress. Get into "**The Search**," seeking confidence in God as your refuge in all situations. Write your answers in the spaces provided.

Take time to "**Respond**," knowing God's Spirit empowers you to trust in Him. Then pray together, bringing your needs before God's throne of grace.

Before the next session, do the "**Do**," recording your thoughts and experiences in the journal page following this session, filling in the prayer page (or using it as a way to pray each day).

Where Am I Now?

Describe what you see as a refuge or fortress—a place where you are safe and strong. Draw a picture of your fortress or use words to tell about it. What things might you find in your place of refuge? If you like, tell why you need such a refuge now.

God's Victories for Anna

1. Anna was a prophetess, one of a handful of biblical women identified as such and the first one, either prophet or prophetess, mentioned in the New Testament. Biblical prophets interpreted the present, foretold the future, and were the voice of God for His people. We are not told in what prophetic capacity Anna served, but we are told that she "did not depart from the temple, but served God with fastings and prayers night and day" (Luke 2:37 NKJV). Read Luke 2:36–38 to discover more about Anna. What do these verses tell you about her?

2a. Biblical authorities cannot tell from these verses whether Anna had been a widow for 84 years or if she was a widow 84 years old. But the verses do hint at some of the struggles and battles Anna must have faced during her life. What may Anna have gone through in her younger years when she lost her husband? How did she respond to that crisis in her life? Where did Anna find refuge? Why do you think she chose that refuge?

2b. What are some crises you have faced or are facing? How did (do) you respond? Where do you find refuge? Why do you choose that refuge? Is your refuge secure? Will it be moved?

3a. What do these few verses tell you about Anna's relationship with God? Write one or two descriptive

words that tell what kind of woman you think Anna was. If you could ask Anna any question about her relationship with God, what would you say?

3b. Think of older persons you know or have known. What do you know about battles they have faced or are facing? How did (do) they react? What does that say about their relationship with God? about the refuge they have? Describe them in one or two words. What about their life would you like to model?

God's Refuge for Anna

4a. In biblical times, fasting was generally done in connection with repentance for sin. Why do you think Anna, who seems not to have been a sinful woman, spent her days (and nights) in fasting and prayer?

4b. The New King James Version (NKJV) says Anna "served God" with fastings and prayers. How might fasting and praying be a service to God? How might fasting and praying be a refuge?

4c. In what ways do you serve God? Why do you choose those ways for service? In what ways is your service to God a refuge that God has provided for you?

5a. Anna knew that her refuge was in God. Turn to

Psalm 46 and discuss what verses might have been especially meaningful for Anna.

5b. As Anna reflected on what God had done for Israel in the past and beheld the Baby Jesus in Mary's arms, what could she say with certainty of her future? (Read Luke 2:38.) of Israel's future?

God's Refuge for Us

6a. What keeps us from seeking refuge in God? Why do we sometimes stand within the tempests of life and refuse to "come out of the rain"? How does the Lord lead us to seek His refuge?

6b. "God is our refuge and strength, an ever-present help in trouble" (Psalm 46:1). When the earth quakes beneath our feet, when the chaos of problems overwhelm us, when we are desolated with our sin or the sin of others against us, we can know that God is immovable, that the Lord Almighty is with us, that the God of Jacob is our fortress. Read Psalm 46 aloud, then describe the refuge that you have in God.

Respond

Reread Luke 2:38. Anna responded to the Child in Mary's arms with thanks to God and joyful confidence to others that this Baby was the final refuge, the refuge

of all ages, the promised Messiah. Write a few words that tell what Anna may have said to those who longed for the Savior. Then write a few words to describe your response to the Messiah and what you might tell others about Him.

In pairs or trios, share your response. Then pray as a group, asking the Lord to give you the confidence Anna had in Him as her refuge, her joy, her Messiah. Include petitions of care and concern for others expressed in today's study. Conclude by saying together the words of Psalm 46:11: "The LORD Almighty is with us; the God of Jacob is our fortress."

Do

This week ask the Lord to help you become more aware of times when He is your refuge—from stress, from guilt, from little things that get you down. Recall the place of refuge that you have described and picture God there to welcome you. Record these times and events in the journal page here.

Additional Bible readings for this week: Numbers 35:5–15; Ruth 3:1–14; and Psalm 16. Copy and attach to a mirror or other place you see daily the words of Deuteronomy 33:27a.

Use the prayer starters each day as you come to the Lord in your quiet time, either writing in your own endings to the sentences or leaving them blank to be used in a new way each day.

For next week, read about Martha in John 11:1–27. Read through and think about Session 3, filling in any responses as you like.

Journal Page

O Lord, You are so _____
_____
_____

and I am so _____
_____
_____
_____

Please forgive me for _____
_____
_____
_____
_____

Help me _____
_____
_____
_____

Please bless and take care of _____
_____
_____
_____
_____

Thanks, Lord, for _____
_____
_____
_____
_____

Martha's Refuge

Where Are We Going?

We will look at Martha of Bethany to see how she recognized God as her refuge, even in the face of death, and that her faith was strengthened as she waited for God's answer; we will see that we too can have the same confidence with which Martha spoke.

Ready, Set, Go

Begin with prayer. Ask God to help you see His answer to your waiting, to help you wait for His answers, and to strengthen your faith as you wait.

Spend a few minutes on "**Where Am I Now?**" Talk about things for which you wait. Get into "**The Search,**" knowing God's Spirit guides and leads your discussions. Write your answers and reflections in the spaces provided.

Take time to "**Respond.**" Realize that God waits too for His children to turn to Him in trust. Then pray together, knowing God hears and answers.

Before the next session, do the "**Do.**" Record your thoughts and experiences in the journal page following this session and fill in the prayer page (or use it as a way to pray each day).

Where Am I Now?

Make a list of and discuss things for which you have waited or are waiting. Place a star or asterisk by the things that take the most patience in waiting.

The Search

The Need

1. Lazarus was dying. Lazarus—the dearly loved brother of Mary and Martha. The two women did the only thing they could. They sent a message to Jesus: "Lord, the one You love is sick" (John 11:3). These were sisters who lived in Bethany (see the reverse study of this book for "Martha's Storms"). They were Jesus' friends and claimed a closeness with the Master few else knew. They owned the home where Jesus and His friends often came to rest and be refreshed. Note that the sisters did not ask Jesus to come. They simply send word, "The one You love is sick." Why do you think they did so when they doubtless had many other friends (see John 11:37) who could comfort them? React to the wording of the message: *The one You love.* Why do you think they didn't say, "The one who loves You"?

2a. Read and record Jesus' response to these dear friends (John 11:4–6). Verse 5 says, "Jesus loved Martha and her sister and Lazarus." Why do you suppose Jesus delayed going to Bethany? Why do you think Jesus said that this sickness would not end in death, but yet Lazarus died?

2b. Why do people become ill and die today? Why do Christians suffer from disease and old age and death?

20

3a. When they sent the message to Jesus, what refuge were Martha and Mary seeking? What do you think they hoped? Why? Do you think they expected Jesus to come? What might they have felt when Jesus did not appear as soon as they thought?

3b. Put your own name into verse 5: "Jesus love[s] …" And yet, at times we tell Jesus our problems and no answer seems to come. Why do you suppose Jesus delays His answers to us? When delays to prayers happen, how do you react? What do you do?

Jesus Is the Answer

4a. It was only after Jesus knew that Lazarus had died that He invited His disciples to travel with Him back to Judea. When He arrived Martha went out to Him. Read of their meeting in John 11:21–27. How is Martha's faith in Jesus evident in how she first greets Him? How is the weakness of her faith evident?

4b. How do you greet answers that Jesus brings you? How do you show evidence of your faith in Him as your refuge from all problems?

5. But sometimes doubts are mixed in with our faith. How does our wishing for "what might have been" get in the way of our belief? In what areas does your faith need to be strengthened? How can this happen? (See Psalm 119:28; Isaiah 41:10; Romans 1:11–12; and Ephesians 3:16.)

Jesus doesn't scold or explain. He simply tells Martha, "Your brother will rise again." And Martha proclaims her belief in the final refuge for all believers: "I know he will rise again in the resurrection at the last day." Read aloud Jesus' response and Martha's confession of faith in John 11:25–27.

6a. Jesus had something else in mind—something for the here and now, something to bring glory to God. Read John 11:35–46. In what way did this miracle meet (or surpass) Martha's and Mary's needs? How did it meet the needs of others? How did it bring glory to God (see v. 45)?

6b. God always answers our prayers in ways that are best for us, in ways that bring Him glory, and in ways that further His kingdom. Think of ways in which the Lord has answered your prayers of need and refuge. How did His answers meet your needs? bring Him glory? meet the needs of others? bring about good for His kingdom?

Respond

Turn to Psalm 46 and choose verses that might have special meaning for Martha. Read aloud any verses that would convey her trust and confidence in Jesus' power and the power of the resurrection. Share words of your own that might have expressed Martha's reaction to Jesus' answer to her waiting.

Now read aloud any verses in the psalm that express your trust and confidence in God's power in every area of your life, in times of waiting for God's answers, and in the power of the resurrection.

Close with prayer. Simply tell the Lord the things that trouble you, and bring your concerns of waiting for God's answers to His throne of mercy and love. Include any worries or troubles expressed throughout the session, knowing God will answer in ways that are best for you and for His kingdom.

Do

This week be aware of times when God is answering your prayers and of times when He asks you to wait. Look for times when He shows that He is your refuge and ways in which His answers bring Him glory and good for His kingdom. Record these in the journal page.

Additional Bible readings for this week: Psalm 5; Jeremiah 29:11–14; and John 14. Copy and attach to a mirror or other place you see daily the words of John 14:16.

Use the prayer starters each day as you come to the Lord in your quiet time, either writing in your own endings to the sentences or leaving them blank to be used in a new way each day.

For next week, reread Psalm 46. Then read through and think about Session 4, filling in any responses as you like.

Journal Page

_____

_____

_____

_____

_____

_____

_____

_____

_____

_____

_____

_____

_____

_____

_____

_____

_____

_____

_____

_____

_____

_____

_____

_____

_____

_____

_____

O Lord, You are so _____

_____

_____

_____

and I am so _____

_____

_____

_____

Please forgive me for _____

_____

_____

_____

_____

Help me _____

_____

_____

_____

_____

Please bless and take care of _____

_____

_____

_____

_____

Thanks, Lord, for _____

_____

_____

_____

_____

Session 4
God's Refuge; God's Victory

Where Are We Going?

We will take a deeper look today at Psalm 46 to discover the quietness of God; to find out how we can be still and know that God is God; to exalt God as our strength and fortress.

Ready, Set, Go

Begin with prayer. Ask God to come to you in the quietness of your study, to open His Word to you through His Spirit so that you might know that He is God.

Spend a few minutes on "**Where Am I Now?**" Think about the quiet times of your day. Get into "**The Search**." Dig into the Word, ready to have God reveal His strength and power in it for you.

Take time to "**Respond**," concentrating on God and who He is. Then pray together, lifting your hearts and voices to the Lord.

Before the next session, do the "**Do**," recording your thoughts and experiences in the journal page following this session, filling in the prayer page (or using it as a way to pray each day).

Where Am I Now?

Describe the quietest part of your day. On a scale of 1 to 10, with 1 being the quietest and 10 the loudest, mark on the chart where your mornings are (A.M.); your afternoons (P.M.); your evenings (E); and your nights (N). Spend a few minutes discussing why you placed your marks as you did.

The Search
The Noise

In the book *The Magician's Nephew*, C. S. Lewis describes the creation of Narnia, a mythical other world, where Aslan the lion typifies Jesus and sings Narnia into being. In beautifully descriptive words, Aslan's songs brings forth flowering trees, winging birds, rushing rivers, thrashing fish, and grunting, squealing, honking, trumpeting, and barking animals. From a peaceful, almost too-quiet atmosphere, the world suddenly hums and buzzes and squawks in joy. With Lewis's words, it's easy to picture the creation of our own world and the great holy gladness God took in forming and bringing forth thriving, bustling, lively creatures. God must not only have rested on the seventh day, but also surely took joyful pleasure in the works of His hands.

How devastating it must have been for all creation when sin entered the world and the joyful noises turned into the clash of rebellion and the crash of death.

1. Read Psalm 46:1–3. What descriptive words does the psalmist use to portray the tumult caused by sin? What kinds of noisy tumult do you see in the world today? Describe a noisy time in your own life.

2a. In the very first verse, however, we are told that God is our refuge and strength. How was He a refuge for Jehoshaphat? for Anna? for Martha? at other times for the children of Israel?

2b. How have you found God to be a personal refuge for you in the last few weeks of this course?

27

The River

Jerusalem is built on a high rocky hill with no rivers running through it. King Hezekiah either built or renovated a tunnel to bring into the city the water from a natural spring found outside the eastern wall. The tunnel brought the water from the spring into the Pool of Siloam and thus supplied the city with water in case of siege. Read Psalm 46:4–7.

3a. The natural spring, called *Gihon* (gusher), formed a river into Jerusalem, a river of running or "living" water. Why are running waters necessary in a siege? What other blessings do running waters bring? What other scriptural accounts include running water or rivers of water?

3b. Read John 4:10–14. What does this say about living water? Why is Jesus, our living water, necessary when our lives are under siege? What other blessings does He give?

4a. "God is in the midst of her [the city], she shall not be moved" (Psalm 46:5 NKJV). This verse says that though everything else is in tumult, the city of God will not be moved—because God is in her midst. In what ways will God not be moved? How did Jehoshaphat discover this? How did Anna rely on this? What did this mean for Martha?

4b. In what ways will the Christian church today not be moved? Why? What does this mean for you? for your faith?

5a. Read Psalm 46:8–11. How does God make wars to cease? Why do you think He needs to "break" and "shatter" and "burn" (v. 9) in order to bring about the end of wars?

5b. Picture the outside of a fortress, strong, stalwart, and immovable. God is that fortress for you, keeping you safe within. What battles does God fight for you? How does He do so?

Think of the greatest violence of all times: the beating, the scourging, the piercing, the agony, the death of Jesus. God's justice demanded perfect atonement for sin. Only through Jesus' perfect life, His violent death, and His glorious resurrection was God able to put an end to the results of sin: eternal damnation and everlasting separation from Him. How much God loves you and me!

6a. Psalm 46:10 reads, "Be still, and know that I am God." What do you suppose the psalmist is saying here? Why do nations need to "be still and know" that God is God? How is God exalted among the nations now? How will He be exalted at the end of the world?

6b. Why do we need to "be still and know" that God is God? How will you exalt God in your own life? with family? with friends? in your neighborhood or community? in your church?

Respond

"Be still and know" that God is God for a period of two or three minutes of absolute silence. Exalt God in your mind. Meditate on His greatness and power, His strength for you, and His claim on you. Then begin quietly sharing with one or two others the magnitude of God. Let this swell to joyful praise as you exalt God together. Finally say together two or three times, "The LORD Almighty is with us; the God of Jacob is our fortress" (Psalm 46:11). Or sing "A Mighty Fortress Is Our God," Martin Luther's great Reformation hymn, which is based on Psalm 46.

Then pray together. Bring any concerns mentioned during the study to God, your fortress, knowing that in Him you have refuge for today and refuge for eternity.

Do

During this week use your journal page to record the quiet times that God speaks to you. Focus on His power and glory. Let His grace and love fill you so that you, with all nations, exalt Him above all.

Additional Bible readings for this week: Psalm 2; Zechariah 2:1–13; and Revelation 21:1–7. Copy and attach to a mirror or other place you see daily the words of Psalm 46:10.

Use the prayer starters each day as you come to the Lord in your quiet time, either writing in your own endings to the sentences or leaving them blank to be used in a new way each day.

May God bless you as you continue regular Bible reading, prayer, journaling, and worship in your walk with Him, your refuge and fortress.